PAMPHLETS ON AMERICAN WRITERS • NUMBER 33

UNIVERSITY OF MINNESOTA

⤙ *Ellen Glasgow*

BY LOUIS AUCHINCLOSS

UNIVERSITY OF MINNESOTA PRESS • MINNEAPOLIS

Distributed to high schools in the United States by
McGraw-Hill Book Company, Inc.

New York   Chicago   Corte Madera, Calif.   Dallas

PUBLISHED IN GREAT BRITAIN, INDIA, AND PAKISTAN BY THE OXFORD
UNIVERSITY PRESS, LONDON, BOMBAY, AND KARACHI

FOR J. DONALD ADAMS

LOUIS AUCHINCLOSS, the author of many novels, short stories, and articles of literary criticism, also wrote the pamphlet *Edith Wharton* in the series of University of Minnesota Pamphlets on American Writers.

⤳ *Ellen Glasgow*

Ellen Glasgow's parents combined the qualities that gave to both antebellum and reconstructed Virginia its stubborn romanticism and its peculiar strength. Her father, of Valley stock, was an ironworks executive and a Scotch Presbyterian in every nerve and sinew; he gave his children all the things they needed but love, and in eighty-six years never "committed a pleasure." The best his daughter could say of him was that he had not hurt anyone for the mere satisfaction of hurting. Her mother, on the other hand, descended from Randolphs and Yateses, was a flower of the old Tidewater, who, smiling in the constant sadness of her tribulations, would have divided "her last crust with a suffering stranger." Miss Glasgow attributed the lingering, undiagnosed malady of which her mother ultimately died to the exhaustion of bearing ten children and the hardships of war and reconstruction, but it was more probably the result of the same nervous temperament that her daughter inherited. "Born without a skin," the young Ellen's Negro mammy, shaking her head, used to say of her charge.

But in 1873, the year of her birth, the worst, at least financially, was over. The Glasgows had, in addition to a town house in Richmond, the farm of Jerdone Castle where their daughter could range over wide fields, the greater part of which were left to run wild in broomsedge and scrub pine and life-everlasting, and cultivate the love of natural things and the sense of kinship with birds and animals that were never to leave her. Too nervous to go regularly to any school, she educated herself by reading all the books in the family library, science and history as well as fiction

5

and poetry. An older sister's husband, a scholar, made her study *The Origin of Species* till she knew "its every page." According to her posthumous and by no means modest memoirs, she seems as a young woman to have had her cake and swallowed it, for she "won all the admiration, and felt all the glorified sensations, of a Southern belle" while at the same time making acquaintance with the squalor of Richmond slums as a worker for the City Mission and becoming a "Fabian Socialist." One can assume, at least, that she was no ordinary debutante.

When her mother died in 1893 she was so prostrated with grief that she tore up the uncompleted manuscript of her first novel, *The Descendant*, and a year passed before she was able to turn back to writing. Something of the same paralyzing prostration was to follow, in later years, the deaths of her sister Cary and of the man described in her memoirs as "Gerald B——." Miss Glasgow always regarded herself as a uniquely sensitive and unhappy person. Answering the question of how she had liked her life in 1934 she replied: "not one day, not one hour, not one moment — or perhaps, *only one* hour and one day." It was true that on top of the nervous headaches and attacks of her youth was loaded the burden of increasing deafness, but she was given the compensations of looks, wit, charm, gaiety (she was never one to wear her melancholy on her sleeve), friends innumerable, and a talent that was to grow in power through a long life almost to the end. She never married, but this was for no lack of opportunity. She broke two engagements and recorded that the maternal instinct, sacred or profane, had been left out of her nature.

Nor was she neglected by the reading public. Again and again she was a best seller. But the delay in the serious critical recognition to which she regarded herself as entitled rankled deeply. Believing that she was leading a literary crusade away from a sterile romantic tradition toward the presentation of the South in a realist manner, lightened by irony, she found it hard to be crossed off as a sentimental regionalist. That she obviously loved her native state and that her books sold by the thousands were perhaps enough to make her seem to the casual eye like the very thing that she abominated. And when she did break through the literary barriers with *Barren Ground* in 1925, she was already in her fifties and beginning to have a nostalgic eye for the old state of society against which she had rebelled. If she shuddered at Thomas Nelson Page, she shuddered more at *Sanctuary*. She might almost have said at the end, like that disillusioned Victorian, Rhoda Broughton: "I began life as Zola; I finish it as Miss Charlotte Yonge."

From the beginning she never wavered in her conviction that her role in life was to write novels — important novels. She kept a sharp eye on every development of her career, including all steps of publication, to ensure the unhampered growth of her reputation as a major novelist. She left Harper, which had published her first two novels, without a qualm (so far as appears in her correspondence) when she decided that Walter Hines Page at Doubleday would do a better job on the third, and after Doubleday had published sixteen of her titles (including a volume of poetry and another of short stories) she left it for Harcourt, Brace because she concluded that much of the Doubleday promotion which had helped to make her famous was "cheap." Similarly, although never rich, she did not hesitate, in the depths of the depression, to turn down an offer by *Good Housekeeping* of $30,000 to serialize *The Sheltered Life,* and she made a habit of seeking out critics to have the chance to present her literary case personally and to make perfectly clear what her books were about. In short, she was Ellen Glasgow's own best agent, as Amy Lowell had been Amy Lowell's.

Her first two novels, *The Descendant* (1897) and *Phases of an*

Inferior Planet (1898), bristle with the young liberal's determination to be shockingly realistic and seem a bit jejune to modern eyes, but it should not be forgotten what a determined step away from romantic fiction, particularly on the part of a young woman gently bred, they must have represented to her contemporaries. If a southern lady produced novels at all, they were expected to deal with plantation life, either in its antebellum splendor or in heroic and picturesque decay. Miss Glasgow's first two tales may seem as far from Faulkner as the sentimental tosh from which they were a reaction, and she herself in later years came to regard the so-called "honest" school of southern literature as a combination of everything that was "too vile and too degenerate to exist anywhere else," but there was nonetheless a strong historical link between the two.

It is a pity that she chose to lay the scene of both these novels in New York which she knew then only as an occasional visitor. Even later, when she had lived in the city for several years in succession, she never caught its flavor as she caught that of Williamsburg, Petersburg, and Richmond. She objected to being labeled a Virginia writer, and, indeed, her truths were universal, but it was still the case that they were better seen against a Virginia background. This, however, was to be no serious limitation, for hers was a diverse state, and she knew it thoroughly, its cities and its rural areas, its aristocrats and its businessmen, its politicians and its farmers. If she was a regionalist, she was a regionalist on a Trollopian scale.

The style of these early books combines the epigrammatic with the sentimental in a way that suggests a mixture of Meredith and Charlotte Brontë. Clever sentences like "Conscience represents a fetich to which good people sacrifice their own happiness, bad people their neighbors' " are to be found with such others as "It was the old, old expiation that Nature had demanded and woman paid since the day upon which woman and desire met and knew each other." Even more awkward is the intrusion into the supposedly free and easy life of the young bohemian characters of certain undiscarded standards of the author's Richmond upbringing. The radical hero of *The Descendant*, who preaches against marriage, is nonetheless still chaste when he meets and falls in love with an emancipated virgin to whom he protests: "I am not worthy to touch the hem of your garment." And Algarcife in *Phases of an Inferior Planet*, who loses his job in a women's college because of his articles on the "origin of sex," can still condemn his wife to bitter need rather than let her supplement the family income by taking a role in light opera. In bitter need, too, be it noted, they still have a "slipshod maid of work."

The important thing, however, to be observed about these forgotten little books is that, for all their crudenesses, they demonstrate a flow of narrative power and a vitality that show a young writer bound to make her mark. *The Descendant*, published anonymously, was by many attributed to Harold Frederic, which seems a greater compliment today than Miss Glasgow thought it at the time. In her middle twenties she was already established and could write Mr. Page about her third novel: "If the gods will it to be my last I don't want people to say 'she might have done big things,' because I am writing this book not to amuse, or to sell, but to *live*, and if it does so I shall be content not to — after it is finished."

The Voice of the People (1900), indeed, marks the real beginning of her career as a novelist. She had already conceived her master plan of writing "in the more freely interpretative form of fiction" a social history of Virginia from the decade before the Confederacy. Possibly using a bit of hindsight and showing that passion to see a lifework as centralized that characterizes the great French novelists, she later classified her fiction as fitting into the following categories and covering the following chronological periods:

History: *The Battle-Ground*, 1850–65; *The Deliverance*, 1878–90; *The Voice of the People*, 1870–98; *The Romance of a Plain Man*, 1875–1910; *Virginia*, 1884–1912; *Life and Gabriella*, 1894–1912.

Novels of the country: *The Miller of Old Church*, 1898–1902; *Barren Ground*, 1894–1924; *Vein of Iron*, 1901–33.

Novels of the city: *The Sheltered Life*, 1910–17; *The Romantic Comedians*, 1923; *They Stooped to Folly*, 1924; *In This Our Life*, 1938–39.

Actually, the only common denominator of all these novels is the Commonwealth of Virginia, as the only one that links the masterpieces of Zola's *Rougon-Macquart* is France in the Second Empire, but at least Miss Glasgow had the wisdom to rest her case on geography and did not try to connect her characters through the branches of an immense and exotic family tree.

The Voice of the People, although third in the history series, was the first to be published, because, unlike *The Battle-Ground* and *The Deliverance*, it required no research. Battle Hall might have been the Jerdone Castle of Ellen Glasgow's own childhood, and we meet her for the first time as a writer in full possession of her native materials. She was to make Virginia the setting of all her subsequent novels but two: *The Wheel of Life* and *Life and Gabriella*. The first takes place totally in New York and is a total failure; the second takes place partly in New York and is in that part a failure. Without the Virginia that Miss Glasgow knew as a historian and felt as a poet, her characters never become fully alive.

As one first begins to succumb to the fascination of Battle Hall, with the visiting aunt who comes for a week and stays for years, with the miraculous reorganizing domestic powers of Miss Chris, with the friendly darkies and the long, succulent meals, with the rumbling memories in sleepy afternoons of more heroic days, one may start up and ask: How is all this so different from the romantic tradition? Isn't this more of Thomas Nelson Page? Perhaps. Miss Glasgow had a deeply ingrained sympathy for the antebellum aristocracy, but at the same time one begins to perceive the parts of the picture that her realist eye picks out: General Tom sinking into sloth and fantasy and the rigid standards of Mrs. Webb operating to depress and freeze people in their born stations. Nicholas Burr, the hero, of the poor white class, may educate himself, like Akershem in *The Descendant*, and may even rise to become governor of Virginia, and die a martyr's death holding off a lynching mob, but he fails to win Eugenia Battle, and his failure has been foreordained by the blind prejudice of her family.

Miss Glasgow's resolution of the class problem, however, is a bit muddied by her own preconceptions. One is willing to accept the fact that Nicholas Burr, like Akershem, is subject to violent fits of rage, and even to accept his rages as attributes of the uncivilized barbarian lurking in all of us, but one cannot as easily accept Miss Glasgow's complacent assumption that such violence lurks more insidiously in the lower orders. Why would not *any* man explode against a heroine who, without a hearing, blandly condemns him for the seduction of a farm girl who has in fact been seduced by the heroine's own brother? Yet Eugenia appears to have the author's sympathy when she finds in Nicholas' fury a "sinister" reminder of his father. And why sinister? Is his father an evil man? No, simply a vulgar one. Certainly there is here a tendency to equate violence with low birth and sex appeal, for the heroes of these early novels, however ugly of temper, have also some of the attributes of supermen. Later on, after a disillusioning personal experience, the men with whom Miss Glasgow's

11

heroines become involved (no longer heroes by any stretch of the term) are weak, self-indulgent, and faithless. The confusion that exists in *The Voice of the People* was ultimately cleared up, but at the expense of the male sex.

Throughout this initial period of her literary career, Ellen Glasgow's hearing was steadily failing. As her income increased she began pilgrimages all over the world "more hopeless than the pilgrimages to shrines of saints in the Dark Ages," for there was no cure for the hardening in the Eustachian tube and the middle ear. Science had failed her body, she complained, as ruinously as religion had failed her soul, and she had to fall back on a humane stoicism and — ultimately — on golf. Deliberately she built "a wall of deceptive gaiety" around herself and cultivated the "ironic mood, the smiling pose." There was a surer refuge in mockery, she found, than in too grave a sincerity.

Romanticism, however, was still evident in *The Battle-Ground* (1902) which Alfred Kazin has called a "superior sword and cape romance based on the legend that the Civil War was fought between gentlemen and bounders." It is the only Glasgow novel where the action takes place before and during the Civil War and consequently before the author's own memory, which may explain why the early chapters are so filled with frothy chatter and gallantry, with toasts and boasts ("To Virginia, the home of brave men and of angels"), with loving loyal slaves and proud, high-tempered colonels. Of course, Miss Glasgow may have been deliberately intensifying the cavalier atmosphere in order to heighten the drama of the coming conflict that would sweep it all away. It has become the classic method of handling the opening of the Civil War, as seen in Margaret Mitchell's *Gone with the Wind* (a book which Miss Glasgow admired) and in Stephen Vincent Benét's *John Brown's Body*. It is, indeed, almost a literary convention to show the Confederacy dancing its way into disaster.

She did better, however, in the war chapters. Here she kept away as much as possible from battle scenes, for she never liked to write about things that she had not seen with her own eyes, and she concentrated on pictures, such as that of wartime Richmond, where her own hard research and contemporary knowledge could combine to give a proper focus. The novel ends where her real work in fiction begins: at the end of the war when the South faces the future in defeat. It is here that she establishes herself as totally distinct from those novelists who could only lament what had passed away and sigh over characters who did the same. Dan Montjoy, coming back to the ruins of his ancestral home, wounded and half-starved, can yet reflect that the memory of a beaten slave which used to haunt him need bother him now no more. And his grandfather, Major Lightfoot, who is unable mentally to take in the fact of Appomattox, augurs the postwar southern mental evasiveness about which Miss Glasgow was to have so much to say and to the exposure of which she was to devote her ironic art.

The Deliverance (1904) is her first fully mature work. It is a well-organized centripetal novel about impoverished aristocrats and unscrupulous parvenus in the era of reconstruction. For the first time Miss Glasgow was able to make effective use of the Virginia soil; and the tobacco fields which bring a fortune to Bill Fletcher, the embezzler who has robbed the Blake family of the plantation where he was once overseer, make a perfect setting for the bloody conflict between the still vigorous old order and the already decadent new, and for the terrible revenge of Christopher Blake who deliberately corrupts and destroys the ex-overseer's grandson. Miss Glasgow was to be outdone only by Willa Cather in her handling of rural atmosphere.

In her affection for the Blakes there is still a bit of nostalgia

13

for antebellum days, but the bleak and closely observed present gives the twist of irony to all the memories and stories of that glorious era. The blind Mrs. Blake, whose family and servants together conspire to create in her sickroom the illusion of a victorious South, going so far as to invent names for the Confederate presidents of two postwar decades, is, of course, the symbol of the old South that rejected reality. Her son Christopher, on the other hand, who works in the tobacco fields to support the family, is an example of the aristocrat who has the courage to face and defeat poverty, even though born with the love of ease and the weakness to temptation in his blood, "with the love, too, of delicate food, of rare wines and of beautiful women." Did Miss Glasgow actually believe in the physical transmission of aristocratic characteristics? Evidently so, for Christopher, without education or other advantages, stands out among his fellow farmers as a natural leader. He is another of Miss Glasgow's supermen — he risks smallpox to bury the children of a former family slave — but he is even more irresistible to women than Nicholas Burr because of his noble birth, and when Maria Fletcher sees him, her creator's style slumps suddenly to the level of the lowest potboiler: "All the natural womanhood within her responded to the appeal of his superb manhood."

Maxwell Geismar has pointed out that Ellen Glasgow's novels are among our best sources of information on the southern mind because we can see in them the persistent imprint of primary cultural myths on even a perceptive and sophisticated talent. Miss Glasgow, he feels, for all her compassion and liberalism, could never quite free herself from her admiration of the old aristocracy with all its narrowness and prejudice. It is true. Negroes in her fiction are apt to appear as a carefree, feckless, lovable servant class whose peccadilloes and promiscuities are to be laughed at rather than condemned. In *One Man in His Time* she was actually able to write a whole book on the social problems facing a liberal governor of Virginia without mentioning the Negroes. She belonged, of course, to a generation that was taught to duck the problem in its cradle. But all this does not mean that she was unaware that it existed. Dan Montjoy in *The Battle-Ground* helps an escaped slave; Mrs. Pendleton in *Virginia* forces herself not to see the slave market; Dorinda Oakley in *Barren Ground* is a true friend of her Negro servant; Asa Timberlake in *In This Our Life* defies his family in order to protect a Negro boy from being framed for a crime. In this last episode Miss Glasgow does, if only for a few pages, face up to the fact that otherwise respectable white people may be willing to sacrifice an innocent colored boy to protect a vicious member of their own race. By and large, however, she did not choose to be overly concerned with the problem. She was one who felt that the modern Negro had lost the "spiritual" quality of his forebears, and she evaded the connection between such spirituality and bondage. She had her loves and her loyalties, and even at her most ironical there were certain boats that she was not going to rock.

In 1900 Ellen Glasgow met the man whom she describes as "Gerald B——" in her memoirs, and until his death seven years later she lived "in an arrested pause between dreaming and waking." As with "Harold S——," the other great love of her life, it was a case of opposites attracting. Gerald was a financier and a married man; they could meet only fleetingly and only on her visits to New York. One infers that the relationship was not happy, but it must have had its wonderful moments, and when he died of an inoperable ailment she was completely overwhelmed. If we are to take the relationship of Laura Wilde and Arnold Kemper in *The Wheel of Life*, a novel which she admittedly wrote as an antidote to her sorrow and later confessed to be in part autobiographical, as a picture of herself and Gerald, we thresh up an interesting speculation. Why was this woman, so dedicated to the mind and spirit, twice to fall in love with egocentric and hedonistic philistines? Was *this* what she meant by the indignities of the spirit to which she was so relentlessly subjected? It is difficult to imagine greater ones.

After receiving the news that Gerald was doomed, she records that she went up on a hillside in Switzerland and lay down on the grass where a high wind was blowing. There she had a mystical experience. "Lying there, in that golden August light, I knew, or felt, or beheld, a union deeper than knowledge, deeper than sense, deeper than vision. Light streamed through me, after anguish, and for one instant of awareness, if but for that one instant, I felt pure ecstasy. In a single blinding flash of illumination, I knew blessedness. I was a part of the spirit that moved in the light and the wind and the grass. I was — or felt I was — in communion with reality, with ultimate being. . . ." Something very like this experience was to go into the making of *Barren Ground* and *The Sheltered Life*.

In the terrible years that followed Gerald's death she became engaged to a man with whom she was never in love, but who offered her everything that her love for Gerald missed: "intellectual congeniality, poetic sympathy, and companionship which was natural and easy, without the slightest sting of suspicion or selfishness." Everything, in short, but delight and joy. His letters, those of a poet, stirred in her no greater emotion than gratitude. She asked herself if she had failed because she had preferred the second best in emotion, just as her fellow countrymen so often preferred the second best in literature. Perhaps she had, but the fact that she could see the irony of her situation was the rock on which she would later build her Queenborough trilogy.

In *The Wheel of Life* (1906), conceived in a mystical mood, poet Laura Wilde and her mentor Roger Adams struggle toward the recognition that man's only valid purpose is to identify himself with God and to lose his ego. The pursuit of happiness, even in love — love, in Laura's case, for a man, Arnold Kemper, who, however inconstant, sincerely offers marriage — is simply an invitation to disillusionment and betrayal. This is a theme that will constantly be met again in Ellen Glasgow's work. The most that a woman can expect from love is the opportunity to develop her character by facing inevitable abandonment with fortitude. It is a dreary credo, and enveloped in the somber atmosphere of *The Wheel of Life*, it makes for dreary reading. Laura's collapse into a living death when she discovers that she no longer loves Kemper is so humorlessly described that it engenders no sympathy. And worst of all, this quiet little drama of the soul is played out in New York, with none of the powerfully evoked landscapes of the Virginia novels. Miss Glasgow could never seem to get interested in describing Manhattan. It is always a cold, shadowy island seen only in terms of directions, "east along Sixty-sixth Street," "west to Fifth Avenue." Nor are even the minor characters indigenous. Angela Wilde, who never leaves her house, hovering upstairs like a wraith because she was compromised in her youth, is more Richmond than New York (we will meet her in later Glasgow fiction), and her senile brother who likes to play the flute seems a faded descendant from the gentle family of Dickensian lunatics.

A Virginia setting makes *The Ancient Law* (1908) better reading, but it is again the inferior product of a depressed period. Novels about saints are apt to be tedious, and Daniel Ordway, born in the arid tradition of those austere heroes of George Eliot, Felix Holt and Daniel Deronda, is not made more credible by having been, like another library model, a convict. The end of the book seems almost designed as a parody of nineteenth-century fictional saints. Ordway, having taken upon his own shoulders the guilt of his daughter's forgery, leaves his home a second time in disgrace and travels back to Tappahannock, the town which under an alias he has redeemed and made prosperous (compare *Les Misérables*), just in time to purchase the steel mills from the villain and save them from destruction by a mob of furious strikers to whom he promises fair hours and wages and by whom he is hailed in a final apotheosis. There was a curious streak of the preacher in Ellen Glasgow, quite at odds with her natural skepticism and ironical humor, that tended to seize upon her in her low moments.

The Romance of a Plain Man (1909) finds her happily back on the main avenue of a career which, almost uniquely among those of American writers, was to improve in quality (except for two long hiatuses caused by mental depression) until her old age. For the first and the last time in a novel she adopted the stratagem of the hero narrator, which disembarrassed the author of all problems as to points of view. She violated, however, the literary principle attached to its use: that everything to be told can be naturally told by the narrator. One does not believe, for example, that Ben Starr, who is announced in the title itself as a "plain man" and who has had to make his way up a rough business ladder from lower middle class rags to upper middle class riches, would describe breezes as being "fragrant with jessamine" or air as "heavy with the perfume of fading roses." Nor does one believe that Miss Glasgow ever intended him to sound as fatuous as he does when he notes that "I, the man of action, the embodiment of worldly success, was awed by the very intensity of my love."

Yet Ben's conquest of Sally Mickleborough's world is well described, and the best thing about it is that he can never make himself realize that he *has* conquered it. He feels that he must go on making money for Sally even when he suspects — or ought to suspect — that she wants only his love. But that, of course, is just Miss Glasgow's point: that he isn't really making money for her, but only to prove to himself that he is as good as her aunts and even as good as the great General Bolingbroke. He has been made to feel too deeply his own social inferiority as a child to imagine that it could ever be hidden by anything but a wall of gold. It is thus that materialism engenders materialism; in the end, when there is almost no hope left for the Starrs' happiness, Ben at last sees that the real division between himself and Sally has come "not from the accident of our different beginnings but from the choice that had committed us to opposite ends." It is Ben who ultimately insists on the importance of class as rigidly as Sally's Aunt Mitty Bland who has contemptuously remarked, when urged to concede the physical strength and stature of her proposed nephew-in-law: "What are six feet, two inches without a grand-father?"

Miss Glasgow was very sensitive to social changes; she saw and took it on herself to record that all over the South, as the industrial system displaced the agrarian aristocracy, men like Ben Starr were forging their way into prominence. She was perfectly willing to welcome them and to give them their due, perhaps even more, for she endows Ben with a touch of her old supermen when he knocks down a man whom he finds beating a horse. But she was handicapped in the business scenes by her ignorance of financial matters. Ben's money dealings are misty, which is again the fault of the narrator technique. He cannot talk about things that his creator did not understand, yet one knows that such a man would never stop talking about his big deals. Perhaps if one saw him through the eyes of Sally, who hated business, this part of the book would be more convincing. Edith Wharton, by showing her tycoons only at parties in *The House of Mirth,* was able to conceal from her reader an ignorance of stock exchange matters as deep as, if not deeper than, Miss Glasgow's. The latter should have done some of the research that Theodore Dreiser did for his Cowperwood novels before letting Ben Starr tell his own story.

If Ben Starr has risen, however, the old order has by no means collapsed. Ben's greatest ambition is to rise only as high as General Bolingbroke, a Civil War hero and aristocrat who has turned in his later years to business to lead the South out of defeat. The General, one of Miss Glasgow's most vivid characters (he cannot allow Miss Matoaca Bland to criticize a politician's immoral life because he cannot allow that she should know that it existed), achieves independence from his own caste by sheer success. Having been exalted in war as well as in peace, having been a leader in the old plantation days as well as the smoky industrial new ones, he, alone of the characters, can see how fluctuating and passable are class lines. He can see what Sally's aunts can never see, that Ben Starr will ultimately change his class with his clothes and that only a few old maids will oppose him to the end.

The Miller of Old Church (1911) marks Ellen Glasgow's coming of age, her advent as a major talent in American fiction. It dramatizes the same rise of the lower middle class as *The Romance of a Plain Man*, but it does so more effectively because the scene is laid in a rural area. Miss Glasgow knew a lot more about millers than she knew about financiers. The drama, too, is intensified by the fact that the upper class here is declining. Ben Starr and General Bolingbroke go forward, so to speak, hand in hand, but the Revercombs on the way up meet and clash with the declining Gays. This makes for a better story, though on a more fundamental level it is the soil, as opposed to the cobblestones of Richmond, that gives the deeper interest. The Revercombs triumph over the Gays because they have stronger roots. We have already seen that rural aristocrats can hold their position only, like Christopher Blake in *The Deliverance*, by turning to the land. In making her point Miss Glasgow occasionally allows us a

ella Carr, after a few vivid chapters
of decayed gentlewomen in Rich-
ms of a New Yorker, George Fowler,
in his native city. His charms must
lasgow insists upon them. They are
ugh his magnetism is faintly sugges-
The Wheel of Life and may have
rst see Gabriella and George together
of asides that "In his eyes, which said
ld not read the trivial and common-
George, in the now habitual way of
and Gabriella, with serene faith in her
the management of a flourishing dress
truggle with her old Dominion blood,
nother lowly born superman who has
rescuing an asphyxiated woman and her
rning house.
hing about this novel is that the author's
the notes that she failed to erase. Gabri-
nging herself to accept the Irishman are
oman of her background, but her attitude
whom she meets at Mrs. Fowler's dinners
birth that the author seems to find quite
lasgow as well as to her heroine it is incon-
wler, "with the bluest blood of Virginia in
gard with such artless reverence the social
daughter of a tavern-keeper." If Mrs. Fowler
o, in other words, she should go about it in

ment in World War I and Miss Glasgow's in-
"Harold S——" of the memoirs came at the
ther event helped to get her out of the slump

glimpse of George Eliot and Thomas Hardy looking over her shoulder, and Jonathan Gay's seduction of Blossom Revercomb is a little too reminiscent of both *Adam Bede* and *Tess of the d'Urbervilles.* She was to assimilate more entirely the bleak morality of her great predecessors when she brought her own to its most effective expression in *Barren Ground.*

The Miller of Old Church shows some of the bluntness of style of Miss Glasgow's earlier days, and the omniscient author continues from time to time to obtrude a bit clumsily on the scene. One feels oneself back in the author's workshop on learning, of Abel Revercomb, that "essentially an idealist, his character was the result of a veneering of insufficient culture on a groundwork of raw impulse," or of Molly that "a passing impulse was crystallized by the coldness of her manner into a permanent desire." But in the delineation of Mrs. Gay, Ellen Glasgow was writing as well as she would ever write. It is the revenge of her aristocrats that even slipping they dominate the scene. Mrs. Gay is everything that old Virginia wanted a woman to be — lovely, helpless, indolent, and ignorant, and she conceals behind these qualities an inner force that enchains and destroys all those around her: her brother-in-law, his mistress, her sister Kesiah (a magnificent portrait of an ugly old maid rejected by a world that idolizes beauty), and finally her own son. The last chapter, where after the catastrophe of Jonathan's murder the characters raise their arms in a paean of praise to the wonder of his mother's fortitude, the same mother whose selfishness and prejudice have caused the tragedy, is the first great triumph in Miss Glasgow's use of irony.

The Mrs. Gays of Virginia, however, were not always destructive. Sometimes they were heroic, in which case, poor creatures, they found themselves, by the turn of the century, harmless anachronisms. Such a one is the heroine of *Virginia* (1913), the first of Ellen Glasgow's great tragicomedies. The amazing thing

21

about the character of Virginia Pendleton is that, loyal, sweet, brave, unimaginative, and uncomplaining, she bores everybody but the reader. In this she surpasses Thackeray's Amelia who bores everybody but Dobbin. She is brought up to be the model wife that every southern gentleman was supposed to desire, and may have desired — twenty years before her birth. She admires her husband without comprehending him or without even trying to. She is gentle when a lady should be gentle but capable of a pioneer woman's strength in adversity. Like her old schoolmistress, the embattled spinster Priscilla Batte, she is capable "of dying for an idea but not of conceiving one." She is ignorant, pure, and beautiful, a rose of the Tidewater, but fascinating to meet — in a novel.

From the very beginning of this admirable book, Virginia's parents and teachers are perfectly united in their unconscious aim of turning her into a creature bound to be blighted by the world in which she must live. Her only hope would have been to find a husband (and there were such) who had been in his turn educated to appreciate her type. But, ironically enough, it is old Priscilla Batte herself who, incapable of envisaging any nice young man who would not cherish Virginia, deliberately stimulates the interest of Oliver Treadwell in this finest flower of her educational garden. From the moment she does so the novel moves as relentlessly to its conclusion as if it had been conceived by Flaubert or Zola. Virginia's undiscriminating adoration ends by driving her husband to New York and another woman, and when he has gone she has nothing to fall back on but the same commodious attic of fortitude that sustained her mother through the dreary years of war and reconstruction. But military defeat is easier to bear than desertion, and Virginia's cup is bitterer than her parents'.

She does, however, have one consolation, her son Harry, who in

age, suggests a juvenile. Gabri
describing the desperate life
mond, is captured by the char
marries him, and goes to live
be accepted because Miss G
not otherwise apparent, tho
tive of Arnold Kemper's i
the same source. When we
we are told in the heaviest
enchanting things, she cou
place quality of his soul."
Glasgow men, deserts her,
own capacities, takes over
shop and, after a brief s
marries Ben O'Hara, a
passed the hero's test by
small children from a bu
Another unfortunate
snobbishness is among
ella's difficulties in bri
understandable in a w
toward the newly rich
is based on a pride of
acceptable. To Miss G
ceivable that Mrs. Fo
her veins, should re
activities of the gran
is going to be a sno
a larger spirit!
American involve
fatuation with the
same time, and nei

of this period. It was obviously humiliating for the possessor of an eye so keen to irony to have to turn it on herself and her lover, but turn it she did in the pages of her memoirs. There is nothing sharper or more devastating in all her fiction than the picture of Harold in *The Woman Within.* Everything that she despised most in life — trivial honors, notoriety, social prominence, wealth, fashion, ladies with titles, the empty show of the world — he adored, and she loved him in spite of it for nothing more than a "defiant gaiety" that piqued her interest. Only when, on a Red Cross mission to the Balkans, he had acted out against a background of war horrors his grotesque parody of a Graustarkian romance with Queen Marie of Romania, was she partially cured of her infatuation. But in the despair that followed this episode she took an overdose of sleeping pills, not caring if she lived or died.

She lived, and there was left the war. Even worse for her fiction than her passion for the "pluperfect snob" was her vicarious suffering over distant carnage. This produced her worst novel — if a political tract full of Wilsonian idealism can be called a novel at all. *The Builders* (1919) grew out of the same shrill war feeling that produced Edith Wharton's *A Son at the Front.* David Blackburn, a waxwork Rochester, harangues his child's nurse, Caroline Meade, a rather testy Jane Eyre, on the sad state of the solid South, the evils of the one-party system, and the need for a league of nations. "The future of our democracy," he writes her in his first love letter, "rests not in the halls of Congress but in the cradle, and to build for permanency we must build, not on theory, but on personal rectitude." Angelica Blackburn's wickedness and her success in playing the injured wife provide what little story there is, but even this is spoiled by the clumsy device of having the reader see her first through Caroline's eyes as a noble, suffering creature. It is so manifest that she is not this that we brand Caroline as a ninny, and the central point of view of the novel is hopelessly discredited.

The almost immediate disillusionment that came to so many after the Armistice came to Ellen Glasgow, and one suspects that she was soon a bit ashamed of *The Builders*. Certainly there is no trace of David Blackburn's exalted idealism in *One Man in His Time* (1922). It is not a good novel, but it is at least a novel, and there must have been those who wondered, after its predecessor, if she would ever write one again. Gideon Vetch, the poor white who has risen to be governor of Virginia, is a man who believes that the end justifies the means, but at least he believes in an end, and he dies, assassinated, the victim of the rising underdogs and the static "haves," the second Glasgow hero to suffer a violent end in this high but evidently dangerous office. For the first time in her fiction Miss Glasgow paid serious attention to her points of view and handled them with some degree of subtlety. Vetch is never seen directly, but always through the eyes of others, hostile or admiring, which lends a needed suspense to his story.

Other than Vetch, however, this book, like *Gabriella* and *The Builders*, is thin. One feels that Miss Glasgow shares Corinna Page's feeling about the hero: "She had a sincere though not very deep affection for Stephen." Stephen Culpeper is too much under the influence of his vapid mother to have been the war hero he is reputed. One does not believe that it took such valiance in 1920 for a young man to marry the daughter of the governor of Virginia simply because Patty Vetch's mother had reportedly been a circus rider. And his awakening to human misery after a single tour of the slums of Richmond is a turgid interruption of the story, as is the melodramatic episode when Patty, who does not know she is adopted and thinks her mother dead, visits her "aunt," actually her mother, now a dope fiend. But at least one feels in the pulse of the novel that Ellen Glasgow

26

was emerging from the second period of despond in which she had been so long engulfed.

The best thing about her life was that the best part of it came after the age of fifty. As she wrote herself: "After those intolerable years, all my best work was to come." Her parents were dead, as were Cary and Gerald, and she was largely cured of Harold. She was alone now in the old gray Georgian house with the great tulip poplars at One West Main Street, except for her companion, Anne Virginia Bennett, who had come as a trained nurse and stayed to be a secretary. She regretted the absence of literary life in Richmond, but it was the world in which she had grown up and from which she drew much of her inspiration. It was home, and a home, too, where she was increasingly admired and respected. When she went out to parties, she talked, as she described it, of "Tom, Dick, and Harry," but why not? The real life was within. And what did Tom, Dick, and Harry matter when she was entering the finest part of her career?

Barren Ground (1925) shows the influence of Hardy at last assimilated. Egdon Heath is not more part of the lives of the characters of *The Return of the Native* than is the Piedmont countryside part of the lives of the Oakleys. Its flatness creates the illusion of immensity, and the broomsedge spreads in smothered fire over the melancholy brown landscape to a bleak horizon. The colors are fall colors from autumnal flowers: the crimson sumach, the wine-colored sassafras, the silvery life-everlasting. The Oakleys themselves are "products of the soil as surely as were the scant crops." Joshua looks heavy and earthbound even in his Sunday clothes; for all his scrubbing the smell of manure clings to him; and when Dorinda walks in the October countryside she feels her surroundings so sensitively that "the wall dividing her individual consciousness from the consciousness of nature vanished with the thin drift of woodsmoke over the fields." The inanimate character of the horizon becomes as personal, reserved, and inscrutable as her own mind.

Even the morality springs from the soil, or rather from man's battle with it. The broomsedge is the eternal enemy, always ready to engulf every new farm and field, and men are graded by how they fight it. "For it was not sin that was punished in this world or the next; it was failure. Good failure or bad failure, it made no difference, for nature abhorred both." Jason Greylock, Dorinda's lover in her youth, is weak, and he is broken and finally in dying becomes a lesser thing than the soil; he is identified with a thistle. Dorinda in her fortitude, a Glasgow fortitude built on Jason's desertion, triumphs over the land and builds a dairy farm where the broomsedge was. After the death of her husband, Nathan Pedlar, married for convenience, and of Jason, Dorinda embraces the land anew. Perhaps Miss Glasgow is a bit carried away by her theme here: "The storm and the hag-ridden dreams of the night were over, and the land which she had forgotten was waiting to take her back to its heart. Endurance. Fortitude. The spirit of the land was flowing into her, and her own spirit, strengthened and refreshed, was flowing out again toward life."

Aside, however, from a few such overladen passages and the old habit of dwelling at too great length on her heroine's suffering in abandonment, *Barren Ground* is her finest work. She achieves a greater unity than in the earlier books by strictly limiting the points of view. The central struggle in the story is between Dorinda and the soil, and we see it entirely through Dorinda's mind except when the author intervenes to supplement our picture of the countryside and Pedlar's Mill. In this the technique is not unlike Flaubert's in *Madame Bovary* where, as Percy Lubbock has pointed out, we have to see only two things: Yonville as it looks to Emma Bovary and Yonville as it looks to Flaubert. Actually, there is much less of the author in *Barren*

Ground because Dorinda, unlike Emma, is a woman of enough perception to give us most of the necessary impressions herself.

Miss Glasgow maintained that the Abernethys (Dorinda's mother was an Abernethy), the Greylocks, and the Pedlars were representative of a special rural class, not "poor whites" but "good people" and descendants of English yeomen, who had never before been treated in fiction. She gains greatly in the vividness of her portrayal by not mixing them with characters of other backgrounds. Everyone we see in Pedlar's Mill belongs in Pedlar's Mill like the broomsedge, and the only chapters that mar the otherwise perfect unity of mood in this beautifully conceived novel are those where Dorinda goes to New York to work for a doctor. Manhattan, which provides the only important non-Virginian settings in Miss Glasgow's fiction, is, as usual, fatal to it.

She now embarked on her great trilogy of Richmond, or "Queenborough": *The Romantic Comedians* (1926), *They Stooped to Folly* (1929), and *The Sheltered Life* (1932). The three books do not constitute a trilogy in the sense that they have a continuous plot or even characters in common, but they share a common setting and class, the latter being the old but still prosperous Richmond families, and a spirit of ironic high comedy. They also share — and this is a fault if they are read consecutively — a hero, at least to the extent that the elderly man who is the principal observer in each has a melancholy sense of having missed the real fun in life. It is confusing that they are so alike yet not the same. Miss Glasgow never hesitated to plagiarize herself.

Turning from *Barren Ground* to *The Romantic Comedians* is like turning from Hardy to Meredith, from *The Return of the Native* to *The Egoist*. It is one of the great tours de force of American literature. "After I had finished *Barren Ground*," she wrote in her preface, "which for three years had steeped my mind in the sense of tragic life, the comic spirit, always restless when it is confined, began struggling against the bars of its cage." Never was it to escape to greater advantage. Judge Honeywell, surrounded and tormented by women, is surely one of the most amusing studies in southern fiction. His outrageous twin sister, Edmonia Bredalbane, who wears her scarlet letter as if it were a decoration, his old sweetheart, Amanda Lightfoot, the eternally brave and sweet "good" woman, whose life is a ruin because she could never face a fact, and his dead wife whose image wears a halo of oppressive rectitude, would all keep him from the folly of turning to a girl forty years his junior, but the benighted old fool has had enough of them (who wouldn't?) and wants one joy, one real joy of his own, before the end. The reader knows, everyone knows, even the judge, deep down, knows that this joy will turn to brambles, but he *will* have his way and does. The young wife, Annabel, is just right, too, for she has all the selfishness of youth and all its charm, and we expect her to find her marriage impossible. There is a tragic tone to the book, but it is never allowed to become heavy. The laughter, even when muted almost to a compassionate silence, is still there.

Ellen Glasgow was now in her early fifties and beginning prematurely to suffer from the tendency of so many older people to find youth without standards and to deplore the loss of disciplines in the world about her. It was the same tendency that spoiled so much of the later fiction of Edith Wharton. Miss Glasgow's correspondence is now increasingly full of complaints about the sloppiness and sordidness of modern living and modern literature. She came to look back on her own past, which she had found so stultifying as a girl, with increased nostalgia as she saw the effects of the new liberty of deportment and the new realism of expression that she had herself espoused. Once the note of shrillness, even of petulance, had entered her fiction it could only be lost when, as in *The Sheltered Life* and in the early chapters of *Vein of Iron*, she moved her setting back prior to those ills with which she now saw the world inundated.

They Stooped to Folly is the first of her books to suffer from this lack of sympathy with young people. The youthful characters are hard, angular, and unconvincing. Millie Burden, with the monotony of a minor character in Dickens, repeats over and over that she is "entitled to her life." Mary Victoria is so repellently fatuous and egocentric that she has to be kept off the scene if we are to believe, as the author insists that we shall, in her great influence over other people. And Martin Welding is too weak and self-pitying to cause the havoc he is supposed to cause in female hearts.

The novel as a whole seems like a compilation of discarded sketches from the atelier that produced its happier predecessor. Virginius Littlepage is a small, stuffy version of Judge Honeywell, and nothing happens to him except that he loses his unloved but superior spouse during and not before his chronicle. There is no Annabel for him, only a flirtation with a gay widow that makes him ridiculous but never pathetic. It is impossible to believe in his great love for his daughter Mary Victoria, whose meanness he sees as clearly as does the reader, or in his great sorrow over her obviously doomed marriage to a man whom she has ruthlessly torn from another woman. It is difficult, in fact, for the reader not to feel that all of the Littlepages deserve anything they get.

So what is left? Nothing but epigrams, and even these are repetitive. The characters cannot seem to make their points too often. Millie Burden talks only of her "rights," and her mother only of Millie's need for punishment. Mrs. Littlepage keeps insisting that she has never known her husband to be sarcastic, whereas the reader has never known him to be anything else. And what is the theme of it all? That a woman should not be punished all her life for having lived with a man out of wedlock!

What can Miss Glasgow have thought she was up to? Nobody *is* so punished in the book, except Aunt Agatha, and that was in the ancient past. And nobody in the book thinks anyone *should* be so punished except Mrs. Burden, and she is represented as an absurd anachronism. Why then, in 1929, did the author keep flogging so dead a horse? Is it possible that she was beginning to feel that the age of prejudices had at least had standards? That one could only have ladies if one burned witches?

They Stooped to Folly cleared out the author's atelier of all these rag ends, for the last volume of the trilogy, *The Sheltered Life*, is a masterpiece. "In *Barren Ground*, as in *The Sheltered Life*," she wrote, "I have worked, I felt, with an added dimension, with a universal rhythm deeper than any material surface. Beneath the lights and shadows there is the brooding spirit of place, but, deeper still, beneath the spirit of place there is the whole movement of life." It is not a modest statement, but Miss Glasgow felt that she had worked too hard to have time for modesty, and certainly these two novels have a vibration different from all her others.

Into the double, battered stronghold of the Archbalds and Birdsongs on Washington Street, now all commercial but for them, creeps the fetid smell of the neighboring chemical plant. The smell is more than the modern world that threatens them from without; it is the smell of the decadence that attacks them from within. The sheltered life is also the life of willful blindness; the two families resist change and resist facts. Eva Birdsong, keeping up the queenly front of a Richmond beauty, tries not to see that her husband is a hopeless philanderer. General Archbald, dreaming of a past which he understands, avoids the duty of facing a present which he does not, while his daughter-in-law brings up little Jenny Blair to be a debutante of the antebellum era. Etta, the hypochondriac, lives in a fantasy world of cheap novels and heroes, and Birdsong, in the arms of his Negro mistress, imagines that he still loves his wife. The rumbles of a world war are heard from very far off. Like the smell down the street they do not yet seem to threaten the sheltered lives of the Archbalds and Birdsongs.

The terrible story that follows is seen from two points of view, General Archbald's and Jenny Blair's, those of age and youth. The General's long reverie into his own youth, "The Deep Past," is probably the finest piece of prose that Miss Glasgow ever wrote. The picture of a nauseated child being "blooded" by his sporty old grandfather on a fox hunt is for once without sentiment for the great Virginia days. Like Judge Honeywell and Virginius Littlepage, General Archbald has missed the high moments of life and has been married, like all elderly Glasgow gentlemen, to a good woman whom he did not love. He has been a gentleman and done his civic duty because, in the last analysis, nothing else seemed any better or certainly any finer, but he has a much deeper sense of what is wrong with his world than the other two heroes of the trilogy and a mystic sense that in death he may yet find the ecstasy that he has lost without ever possessing. Under the prosperous attorney and the member in good standing of the Episcopal church is a poet. If he were not quite so old, he might have saved his granddaughter.

But nobody is going to do that. Jenny Blair, brought up in innocence by her gallant widowed mother, cannot believe herself capable of doing anything that is not quite nice. She is drawn into an entanglement with Mr. Birdsong because she will not see that adultery is something that could happen to her. She is a little girl, even at eighteen, a bright, innocent, enchanting little girl, and the subtlest thing in this subtle book is that even while we keep seeing the small events of Washington Street from her point of view, we gradually become aware that others are beginning to see her differently, that John Welch, the Birdsongs' ward, suspects what she's up to, that Birdsong is aware that she's tempting him, that even her mother and grandfather begin to sense a change. The warnings proliferate, and the tempo of the book suddenly accelerates until the vision of Jenny Blair as a sharp-toothed little animal, free of all rules and restraints, reaching out to snatch the husband of her desperately ill friend, bursts upon us in its full horror, just before the final tragedy. Eva Birdsong shoots her husband, and his body slumps in the hall amid the carcasses of the ducks that he has killed. It is the ultimate dramatization of the divorce between the Virginian myth and the Virginian fact, the climax of the novel and of Ellen Glasgow's fiction.

John Welch is the best of youth, as Miss Glasgow was coming to see youth, but he is a dry young man, tough and belligerently unsentimental. In assessing Eva Birdsong's chances of surviving her operation he mentions to General Archbald that her kidneys are sound. It is not, of course, agreeable to this gentleman of the old school to hear a lady's vital organs spoken of as plainly as if they were blocks of wood, but he reflects that perhaps such bluntness is the better way, that "wherever there is softness, life is certain to leave its scar." In this he is certainly the spokesman for his creator who felt that all her life she had been constantly soft and constantly wounded, but there is no question of where her sympathies lay. For all her expressed tolerance of Welch and his contemporaries, they lay with the General, and with her sympathies went the conviction that the suffering life was the richer one.

Two more novels were to follow *The Sheltered Life*, but they show an attenuation of powers. *Vein of Iron* (1935) seems a hollow echo of *Barren Ground*. It starts well enough, for it starts in the past where as an older woman Miss Glasgow was increasingly at home, and deals with people whom she had not treated before, the descendants of the Scotch-Irish settlers in the southern part of the Virginia Valley. This was where her father's people had come from, and she was able effectively to evoke in the early chapters the bare, grim Presbyterian elements of the Fincastle family and their village, called, with a labored appropriateness, Ironside. The characters who are hard are very hard, and those who are stoical are very stoical, and even the names of the surrounding geographical features suggest the somber spiritual atmosphere in which these joyless people live: God's Mountain, Thunder Mountain, Shut-in Valley. Mobs of shrieking children cast pebbles at idiots and unmarried mothers alike, though there are few of the latter, as a girl need only point to the man actually, or allegedly, responsible to have him dragged to the altar by her fellow villagers. It seems possible that Miss Glasgow may have written a bit too much of her father's character into Ironside, but the result is very much alive. Such cannot be said of the second part of the novel where the characters move to Queenborough and to the present. Ada Fincastle becomes a serial heroine, a soap-opera queen.

Consider the list of her wrongs. Ralph McBride is wrested from her by an unscrupulous girl friend and returns, a married man, to make her pregnant. Ironside spits at her, and her grandmother dies of the disgrace. Ralph eventually marries her, but war neuroses have made him moody and unfaithful, and in Queenborough, during the depression, they are reduced to desperate want. Ralph, out driving with the girl next door, is nearly paralyzed in an automobile accident. Yet Ada is always superb; her vein of iron sees her through. The reader must take it on faith. One does not see her, as one sees Dorinda in *Barren Ground*, working on her farm, milking cows, supervising the help, purchasing new fields. Even in *Life and Gabriella* one sees what Gabriella does in her shop, so that one has a sense of the therapy which she applies to her sorrow. But Ada relies simply on her inheritance of character.

The book ends on a harsh note of denunciation of the formlessness and aimlessness of life in the 1930's, a theme that is picked up and enlarged upon in Miss Glasgow's final novel, *In This Our Life* (1941), where the amoralism in which she believed Richmond to have been engulfed seems to have affected not only the young but the old and — one almost suspects — the author herself. For how else can one explain Asa Timberlake?

At first blush he seems in the tradition of Honeywell, Littlepage, and Archbald, those elderly, nostalgic gentlemen who have missed the thrills as well as the substance of life, and like them he has his creator's sympathy. "For the sake of a past tradition he had spent nearly thirty years doing things that he hated and not doing things that he liked; and at the end of that long self-discipline, when he was too old to begin over again, he had seen his code of conduct flatten out and shrivel up as utterly as a balloon that is pricked." But *was* it self-discipline? Asa's life has simply gone by default; he is that commonest of American fictional heroes, the husband dominated by a strong-minded hypochondriac wife. But Asa has none of the dignity of his predecessors in the Queenborough trilogy; he is plotting, with the author's apparent approval, a weak man's escape. As soon as his wife shall have inherited the fortune of a rich uncle, he will quietly decamp with the widow of an old friend. Surely he is as bad as the young folk.

Well, not quite, for they are monsters. Roy, the heroine, and Peter have married with the understanding that either may have back her or his liberty on request. Incidentally, there is a similar bargain between the young couple in Mrs. Wharton's equally disapproving novel, *The Glimpses of the Moon*. Roy's sister, Stanley, ditches her fiancé, Craig, in order to take Peter from Roy, and then, having driven Peter to suicide, she returns to rob her sister a second time, of Craig with whom poor Roy has been consoling herself. During all of these goings-on the four characters, like Asa, are saturated with self-pity. One feels that Miss Glasgow's conviction that men are doomed to weakness and that women can rise above their destiny of betrayal only by stoicism has now reached the pitch of an obsession. Yet she works her plot around the gravely offered thesis that love is vital to the young because it is "the only reality left," though it cannot save them because they treat each other "as if they were careless fellow-travellers, to be picked up and dropped, either by accident or by design, on a very brief journey." But that is not necessarily one's own experience of America in 1938 when the action of the novel takes place.

There are, however, moments. There are always moments, even in the least estimable of Ellen Glasgow's books. When Stanley tries to put the blame of her hit-and-run accident on a Negro boy, and the family prepare to back her up, the novel suddenly soars in stature. Here, at last, is a problem that is real and competently handled, the only time, too, in nineteen novels where Miss Glasgow faces, however briefly, what the South has done to its colored people. And Uncle William Fitzroy, the tycoon whose millions have vulgarized him, despite his genteel background, into the likeness of a noisy parvenu, the forerunner of "Big Daddy" in *Cat on a Hot Tin Roof*, seems to bring Tennessee Williams and Ellen Glasgow into brief but entrancing partnership.

Mention should be made of Miss Glasgow's twelve short stories recently assembled in a volume by Richard K. Meeker. It was not a medium that she much liked or in which she enjoyed much success. She was a discursive writer and needed space to appear to her best advantage. Almost half of the stories deal, as might be anticipated, with the struggle of women with men who are not worthy of them, the theme that underlies so much of her "social history" of the South. As Mr. Meeker amusingly sums it up: "Her typical plot sequence runs: girl meets boy; girl is taken advantage of by boy; then girl learns to get along without boy, or girl gets back at boy."

Best of the tales are four ghost stories, all told in the first person, a method adopted in only one of her novels, but a useful one in helping the reader suspend his disbelief. "Dare's Gift" and "Whispering Leaves" are most effective because of their atmosphere of old Virginia mansions which she knew so well how to evoke; but because in her earlier writing she had no interest in keeping things back, because she seemed, on the contrary, to have almost a compulsion to let her reader know what was on her mind at each moment, she had to remain an amateur in the fiction of the supernatural.

In 1954, nine years after Ellen Glasgow's death of heart disease, her literary executors published under the title *The Woman Within* the memoirs that had been confided to their discretion. There were those who were distressed by this posthumous revelation of the author's self-pity and vanity and who claimed that the memoirs gave a wrong impression of a woman who had always seemed in life so gay and bright and full of sympathy for others. But so long as one bears in mind that this is only Ellen Glasgow as Ellen Glasgow saw her, *The Woman Within* is filled with valuable insights.

It also contains some of her best writing. The pages about "Harold S———," the snob and name-dropper, are as good as anything in *The Romantic Comedians*, and the irony is supplied by the memoirist herself who was in love with the man she despised. How could one get a better glimpse of an author at work than in her description of her meeting with Harold: "I observed him for an instant over my cocktail, wondering whether he could be used effectively in a comedy of manners. My curiosity flagged. What on earth could I find to talk about to a person like that?" What indeed? Yet the association that began that night was to last twenty-one years. So we see the novelist looking for a story and finding one — as ironical as any she wrote — happening to herself. Why, she asks herself in despair, was Harold fated to meet every crisis with a spectacular gesture? "Afterwards, when I read in the 'Life Story' of a Balkan Queen, that, as she said farewell to a Southern Colonel, he had fallen on his knees before her and kissed the hem of her skirt, I recognized the last act of chivalry. So Harold had parted from me when he sailed for the Balkans."

The most valuable thing in the memoirs, however, is the picture of a woman's dedication to her art. From the beginning she had wanted to be a writer above everything, and not just a writer, but specifically a novelist. After the publication of her first book she realized that she needed a steadier control over her ideas and material, a philosophy of fiction, a prose style so pure and flexible that it could bend without breaking. From Maupassant she gained a great deal, but not until, by accident, she happened to read *War and Peace* did she know what she needed. "Life must use art; art must use life. . . . One might select realities, but one could not impose on Reality. Not if one were honest in one's interpretation, not if one possessed artistic integrity. For truth to art became in the end simple fidelity to one's own inner vision." She summed up her artistic credo as follows: "I had always wished to escape from the particular into the general, from the provincial into the universal. Never from my earliest blind gropings after truth in art and truth in life had I felt an impulse to write of a single locality or of regional characteristics. From the beginning I had resolved to write of the South, not, in elegy, as a conquered province, but, vitally, as a part of the larger world. Tolstoy made me see clearly what I had realized dimly, that the ordinary is simply the universal observed from the surface, that the direct approach to reality is not without, but within."

It puts one off a bit that Ellen Glasgow struck, again and again, so high a note for herself. As she conceived of her personal sufferings as more intense than anyone else's, so did she conceive of herself as a novelist on a Tolstoian scale. She did not hesitate, in the preface to *Barren Ground*, to nominate it as the one of her books best qualified for immortality, and in her memoirs she described it further, together with the Queenborough trilogy and *Vein of Iron*, as representing "not only the best that was in me, but some of the best work that has been done in American fiction." In her personal philosophy, and despite a sensitive mind that "would always remain an exile on earth," she believed that she had found a code of living that was sufficient for life or for death. And in her later years she loved to play the queen in the New York publishing world, dangling the possibility of her largesse, half in jest, half in earnest, before the different editors who bid for her books. John Farrar relates that when she made her ultimate decision to go to Alfred Harcourt, the latter went down on his knees before her in her hotel suite like Harold S—— before Marie of Romania. But one can see through the boasting and the jesting, with its aspect of essentially southern horseplay, to her never joking resolution and determination to be a great novelist. One can look back at the young Ellen Glasgow like the young Victoria (to evoke another queen), affirming solemnly her will to be good.

The advantages that she brought to her task and ambition were indeed considerable. Out of her wide reading she selected the mightiest and probably the best models to guide her in her recreation of the Virginia scene. She used Hardy as her master in rustic atmosphere, George Eliot as her guide in morality, Maupassant for plot, and Tolstoi for everything. She had the richest source material that any author could wish, consisting simply of a whole state and its whole history, a state, too, that occupies the center of our eastern geography and of our history and that not coincidentally has produced more Presidents than any other. And the social range among Miss Glasgow's characters is far greater than that of most twentieth-century novelists, suggesting that of such Victorians as Trollope, Dickens, Elizabeth Gaskell, and, again, George Eliot.

She not only considered every social group, but she covered wide varieties within each. In the top ranks of the old hierarchy she showed aristocrats in their glory, such as Major Lightfoot, and aristocrats in their decay, such as Beverly Brooke (in *The Ancient Law*). She showed them turning to the new world of business and dominating it, such as General Bolingbroke, and turning to the same world to be dominated and ultimately vulgarized by it, such as William Fitzroy. She showed aristocrats surviving into our own time, such as Judge Honeywell and Virginius Littlepage, having made the necessary adjustments and compromises, respectable, prosperous, but curiously unsatisfied, and she showed aristocrats like Asa Timberlake, who have been beaten into mediocrity and have failed in life without even the consolation and romance of a picturesque decay. Among the women of this world she created such magnificent anachronisms as Mrs. Blake, such noble, docile, and submissive wives as Virginia Pendleton, such apparently submissive but actually dominating mothers as Mrs. Gay, and such a reconstructed success in the North as Gabriella Carr.

In the middle ranks we find the rising businessman, Ben Starr, the risen politician, Gideon Vetch, the corrupt overseer, Bill Fletcher, the poor philosopher, John Fincastle, the "yeoman" farmers, Dorinda Oakley and Nathan Pedlar, the thriving miller, Abel Revercomb, and, among the lower orders, the "poor white" Burr family, the Starrs from whose midst Ben rises, the victims of the Richmond slums whom Stephen Culpeper is made to visit, the village prostitute and her idiot son in *Vein of Iron*, and, of course, all the Negro servants. Despite what has already been said about the limitations of Miss Glasgow's characterization of Negroes, the servants in her novels are absolutely alive and convincing. In at least one instance, that of the maid and companion to Dorinda in *Barren Ground*, the characterization is as successful as of any of the author's other women.

Miss Glasgow had the same range in scenery that she had in human beings, and she could make the transfer without difficulty from the grim mountains and valleys of *Vein of Iron* to the interminable fields of broomsedge in *Barren Ground* and thence to the comfortable mansions of Richmond and to the smaller gentility of Petersburg and Williamsburg. Highly individual in American letters is her ability to pass with equal authority from country to city, from rusticity to sophistication, from the tobacco field to the drawing room, from irony to tragedy.

Yet for all her gifts and advantages she does not stand in the very first rank of American novelists. She was unable sufficiently to pull the tapestry of fiction over her personal grievances and approbations. The latter are always peeping out at the oddest times and in the oddest places. It is strange that a novelist of such cultivation and such fecundity and one who was also such a student of her craft should not have seen her own glaring faults. How is it possible that the woman who could imagine the brilliant repartee of Edmonia Bredalbane, which annihilates every vestige of pretentiousness in Queenborough, should not have torn up the dreary sermon that is called *The Builders*? How could the author of prose which conveys all the beauty and mystery of the desolate countryside in *Barren Ground* have written the tired purple passages in earlier novels which describe the animal charm of handsome men and women in terms that might have been lifted from the very women's magazines that she so violently despised? How, moreover, could she have failed to see that her own bitterness on the subject of men was reflected in her heroines to the point of warping the whole picture of their lives? The mystery of Ellen Glasgow is not so much how she could be so good a writer as how she could on occasion be so bad a one.

Like Edith Wharton, she will be remembered for her women, not her men. The course of her heroes is a curious one. They start, romantically enough, as men of fierce ideals and raging passions, Byronic in their excesses, impatient of injustice and burning to remake the world. Akershem and Burr are men of the people; the lowness of their origin contributes to their strength, their violence, and their sex appeal. They are a bit lurid, but there will come a time in Miss Glasgow's fiction when we would be glad enough to see them again. With Dan Montjoy in *The Battle-Ground* she inaugurated a period of more respectable, conventional heroes. He is followed by Christopher Blake, Ben Starr, and Abel Revercomb, all of them men of considerable strength and power. But in *Virginia* the weak, selfish, deserting male makes his appearance, and he is to stay through to the end of her fiction. Oliver Treadwell, George Fowler, Jason Greylock, George Birdsong, Peter Kingsmill, Martin Welding, Ralph McBride, and Craig Fleming are all faithless to good women who love them and are all faithless more from the weakness of their characters than the force of their passions. What is most appalling in Miss Glasgow's indictment is that the only ground of redemption that she can find in those of them whom she regards as redeemable, i.e. the last three of the list, is a groveling, lachrymose self-pity. Listen to Martin Welding as his father-in-law interrogates him about the unhappiness of his marriage to Mary Victoria:

"Why don't you tell me about it and let me help you?" the older man asked with all the sympathy that he could summon.

The merest flicker of gratitude shone in the sullen misery of Martin's look. "The trouble is that I have come to the end of my rope. I am wondering how much longer I shall be able to stand it."

"Stand what, my boy?"

"Stand the whole thing. Stand life, stand marriage, stand women."

Mr. Littlepage frowned. "But this isn't normal," he said sternly. "This isn't rational."

"Well, what am I to do?"

"You should see a physician."

"I've seen dozens of them since I met Mary Victoria."

"And what do they say?"

"That I'm not normal, I'm not rational."

"Then, it seems to me, you will have to believe it."

"I do believe it, but that doesn't make it easier. I am still that way no matter what I believe."

The men would not matter so much if they were not taken quite so seriously by the women. Lawrence Selden in Edith Wharton's *The House of Mirth* is a passive spectator hero, but Lily Bart suffers little enough from his preference for the sidelines. Miss Glasgow's heroines, on the other hand, are devastated by her worthless men, and it is just here that her fiction is pulled most seriously out of line. Acceptance of Dorinda Oakley and Gabriella Carr as the towers of strength that they must be to accomplish what they do is difficult to reconcile with the long, tortured passages in which they dwell with the lovingness of hypochondriacs upon their grief. One wonders if their kind of women would not have thrown off disappointment and disillusionment with more dispatch and if Miss Glasgow was not attributing her own sensitivity to natures that had, by definition, to possess tougher fibers. In the final novel the question is reduced to absurdity by Roy Timberlake who succeeds in being abandoned by *two* men and suffers equally at the hands of each.

For all her faults, however, it is hard to get away from the fact that without Ellen Glasgow there would be a great gap in our fiction, particularly where it concerns the South. She was determined to reproduce the South as it was, and although we are conscious today of things added and things omitted, we search in vain for any contemporary or predecessor of hers who even approached her accomplishment. Furthermore, it is astonishing to consider how different in style and mood were her three principal works. *Virginia* might not be worthy of Flaubert, but one suspects that Zola would not have disowned it, nor would Hardy have been ashamed of *Barren Ground*. And any novelist of manners would have been delighted to have produced *The Romantic Comedians*.

Frederick P. W. McDowell has astutely pointed out that Ellen Glasgow's accomplishments and limitations as a writer are best suggested in her own judgment of another southern writer, Edgar Allan Poe: "Poe is, to a large extent, a distillation of the Southern. The formalism of his tone, the classical element in his poetry and in many of his stories, the drift toward rhetoric, the aloof and elusive intensity, — all these qualities are Southern. And in his more serious faults of overwriting, sentimental exaggeration, and lapses, now and then, into a pompous or florid style, he belongs to his epoch and even more to his South."

When Ellen Glasgow began her career, there was almost no serious literature in the South. The pioneer element in her work today is obscured by the fact that the romantic school of southern fiction against which she reacted not only has disappeared but has hardly left a trace. Similarly, the modern school has gone so far beyond her in exploration of the freakish and the decadent that she seems as mild in comparison as Mary Johnston or Amélie Rives. She herself enlarged the distance between her work and that of the southern novelists who were becoming popular in her later years by deriding them. "One may admit that the Southern

States have more than an equal share of degeneracy and deterioration; but the multitude of half-wits, and whole idiots, and nymphomaniacs, and paranoiacs, and rakehells in general, that populate the modern literary South could flourish nowhere but in the weird pages of melodrama." Yet she herself is the bridge, and the necessary bridge, between the world of Thomas Nelson Page and the world of William Faulkner, Katherine Anne Porter, Eudora Welty, and Tennessee Williams.

She will probably not be remembered as the historian of Virginia that she wished to be. This ambition may have been too great for the fiction that she produced. Only four of her nineteen novels, *Virginia, Barren Ground, The Romantic Comedians,* and *The Sheltered Life,* have won more than a temporary place in American letters. But her picture of the South emerging from defeat and reconstruction with all its old legends intact and all its old energy preserved and managing to adapt itself, almost without admitting it, to the industrial exigencies of a new age — like the Bourbons in that it had forgotten nothing, but unlike them in that it had learned a lot — is one that has passed into our sense of American history.

↙ Selected Bibliography

Works of Ellen Glasgow

THERE are two collected editions of Ellen Glasgow's work: the Old Dominion Edition (Garden City, N.Y.: Doubleday, Doran, 1929, 1933) and the Virginia Edition (New York: Scribner's, 1938). Both collected editions include Miss Glasgow's prefaces.

NOVELS AND COLLECTIONS OF SHORT STORIES

The Descendant. New York: Harper, 1897.
Phases of an Inferior Planet. New York: Harper, 1898.
The Voice of the People. New York: Doubleday, Page, 1900.
The Battle-Ground. New York: Doubleday, Page, 1902.
The Deliverance. New York: Doubleday, Page, 1904.
The Wheel of Life. New York: Doubleday, Page, 1906.
The Ancient Law. New York: Doubleday, Page, 1908.
The Romance of a Plain Man. New York: Macmillan, 1909.
The Miller of Old Church. Garden City, N.Y.: Doubleday, Page, 1911.
Virginia. Garden City, N.Y.: Doubleday, Page, 1913.
Life and Gabriella. Garden City, N.Y.: Doubleday, Page, 1916.
The Builders. Garden City, N.Y.: Doubleday, Page, 1919.
One Man in His Time. Garden City, N.Y.: Doubleday, Page, 1922.
The Shadowy Third and Other Stories. Garden City, N.Y.: Doubleday, Page, 1923.
Barren Ground. Garden City, N.Y.: Doubleday, Page, 1925.
The Romantic Comedians. Garden City, N.Y.: Doubleday, Page, 1926.
They Stooped to Folly. Garden City, N.Y.: Doubleday, Doran, 1929.
The Sheltered Life. Garden City, N.Y.: Doubleday, Doran, 1932.
Vein of Iron. New York: Harcourt, Brace, 1935.
In This Our Life. New York: Harcourt, Brace, 1941.
The Collected Stories of Ellen Glasgow, edited by Richard K. Meeker. Baton Rouge: Louisiana State University Press, 1963.

POETRY

The Freeman and Other Poems. New York: Doubleday, Page, 1902.

47

NONFICTION

A Certain Measure. New York: Harcourt, Brace, 1943.
The Woman Within. New York: Harcourt, Brace, 1954.
Letters of Ellen Glasgow, edited by Blair Rouse. New York: Harcourt, Brace, 1958.

CURRENT AMERICAN REPRINT

Barren Ground. New York: American Century (Hill and Wang). $1.95.

Critical Studies

Brooks, Van Wyck. *The Confident Years.* New York: Dutton, 1952.
Geismar, Maxwell. *Rebels and Ancestors.* Boston: Houghton Mifflin, 1953.
Giles, Barbara. "Character and Fate: The Novels of Ellen Glasgow," *Mainstream*, 9:20–31 (September 1956).
Hoffman, Frederick J. *The Modern Novel in America.* Chicago: Regnery, 1951.
Kazin, Alfred. *On Native Grounds.* New York: Reynal and Hitchcock, 1942.
McDowell, Frederick P. W. *Ellen Glasgow and the Ironic Art of Fiction.* Madison: University of Wisconsin Press, 1960. (The only thorough survey of Ellen Glasgow's work, containing an exhaustive bibliography.)
Monroe, N. Elizabeth. *Fifty Years of the American Novel.* New York: Scribner's, 1951.
Rubin, Louis D., Jr. *No Place on Earth: Ellen Glasgow, James Branch Cabell, and Richmond-in-Virginia.* Austin: University of Texas Press, 1959. (Supplement to *Texas Quarterly*, Vol. 2.)